Original title:
Treetop Tales of Laughter

Copyright © 2025 Creative Arts Management OÜ
All rights reserved.

Author: Evan Hawthorne
ISBN HARDBACK: 978-1-80567-300-2
ISBN PAPERBACK: 978-1-80567-599-0

Lively Antics at Bird's Eye View

Squirrels in acorn caps, so proud,
Chasing each other, laughter loud.
A parrot pranks a lazy crow,
Whipping up mischief, oh what a show.

Frogs on high branches, sing a tune,
While raccoons juggle in the afternoon.
With every giggle, the branches sway,
Nature's comedy, brightens the day.

The Heartbeat of the Forest

Buzzy bees dance in the air,
Wobbling branches, a sight so rare.
Chipmunks chuckle under the shade,
Tickling the trees, a grand parade.

A turtle slides on a mossy log,
Giving the frogs quite a shock.
Leaves whisper secrets in delight,
While shadows frolic, taking flight.

Serenade of the Singing Leaves

Leaves hum tunes with the breeze,
Giggling as they sway with ease.
A raccoon tickles a sleeping fawn,
Waking the woods at the break of dawn.

The owls hoot with a wink and nod,
As butterflies dance, completely awed.
Laughter echoes through every tree,
The forest life in harmony.

Winds of Whimsy

Breezes blow through a giggling glade,
Where shadows bounce and frolic, unafraid.
A dog chases his tail, in a whirl,
While butterflies dive and gladly twirl.

Old logs form a stage for a show,
With forest critters taking a bow.
As moons rise high and stars ignite,
Laughter hugs the woods, day and night.

Laughter among the Canopies

In the branches high, chattering birds,
Their silly songs turn whispers to words.
Squirrels chase each, with leaps so grand,
As giggles echo across the land.

Sunbeams dance in a joyful race,
While leaves perform a playful embrace.
A chipmunk prances, it twirls with glee,
Beneath the boughs of the laughing tree.

The Playful Palette of Green

Brush strokes of laughter paint the air,
With every rustle, there's joy to share.
The ferns wave gently, it's quite a sight,
As colors blend in pure delight.

Fluttering leaves like clapping hands,
Celebrate joy in whimsical strands.
A parrot squawks with a cheeky grin,
Spreading cheer where the fun begins.

Revelries in the Woodland Heights

Up in the boughs where the breezes play,
Happy critters frolic through the day.
A deer does a jig, quite out of blue,
While rabbits laugh as they hop askew.

With every splash of sunlight's cheer,
Nature's jesters dance without fear.
The rhythm of joy fills every nook,
As chuckles tickle the old oak's hook.

The Cheerful Arborists

Climbing trees, the laughter rings,
As playful hearts embrace their wings.
With every swing, the world spins round,
Joy hangs heavy, a magical sound.

Blossoms giggle, their petals sway,
While busy bees buzz in a funny way.
The garden thrives on silly pranks,
As nature holds a festive banquet's thanks.

Swaying Branches of Joy

In the breeze, branches giggle,
Leaves dance, and the sky starts to wiggle.
Squirrels scamper, a cheeky ballet,
As sunlight plays, banishing gray.

The parrot squawks a silly cheer,
Echoes tickle the ears with glee.
Acorns fall like raindrops, dear,
The trees are bursting with wild spree.

The Secret Symphony of Foliage

Rustling leaves sing a tune so bright,
Grasshoppers leap in sheer delight.
Bumblebees buzz a hum of bliss,
Nature's orchestra, there's nothing amiss.

Whispers of wind tickle the bark,
A cat and a crow plan a spark.
A turtle smirks in the shade, not shy,
As the sun winks down from up high.

Playful Shadows at Dusk

Shadows twist and jiggle in play,
Nutty raccoons come out to sway.
The moon peeks down with a grin so wide,
As owls hoot tales with pudgy pride.

Fireflies flicker like stars on earth,
In this nighttime caper, there's much mirth.
Under starlight, laughter flows,
As critters share their nighttime shows.

High Above the Ground

Up in the branches, giggles abound,
Swinging from ropes, they leap from the mound.
Kites flutter high, in the golden air,
A kingdom of joy where none can compare.

With each acorn drop, laughter erupts,
In this haven where chaos corrupts.
Every corner hides a fun surprise,
Even the clouds join in the ties.

Arboreal Antics

In the branches, squirrels play,
Chasing each other, come what may.
With acorns flying through the air,
Laughter echoes everywhere.

A parrot squawks a silly tune,
Dances wildly under the moon.
While cheeky raccoons, in disguise,
Make heroes of their clever lies.

The breeze whispers secrets, oh so bright,
As owls chuckle at their flight.
The world above is full of jest,
Where every critter knows their best.

So up we climb to join the fun,
In a leafy world, there's room for one.
With every giggle, every cheer,
We find adventures waiting near.

High Above the Ground

The height brings giggles, oh what a sight,
As monkeys swing with sheer delight.
They toss their hats and flip around,
Creating havoc above the ground.

A fawn peeks out, with a curious blink,
While all around, the tree frogs sing.
They leap and bound, with legs so spry,
Their laughter floats into the sky.

Here comes a raccoon, with sticky paws,
Stealing snacks, with no flaws.
The woodland joins in merry spree,
In this playground of glee and esprit.

With every jump and silly game,
No two rascals are ever the same.
The air is thick with gleeful cheer,
As sunshine glimmers, bright and clear.

Leafy Larks and Skybound Songs

A flurry of leaves, a gust of glee,
Whirling round, come dance with me!
A playful breeze, with ticklish might,
Sways the branches, morning light.

Singing birds take to the sky,
Their laughter echoing, oh so high.
From swing to swing, they're soaring far,
In this jolly world, we raise the bar.

Chipmunks giggle, splashing below,
In puddles of joy, they put on a show.
Just past the bend, adventures blend,
The fun and frolic never end.

With every rustle, and every sound,
Magic happens, joy is found.
So join the frenzy, join the throng,
In leafy larks and skybound songs.

The Joyful Nest

Nestled high, a cozy crowd,
Chirpy chirps, both sweet and loud.
With fluffs and puffs, they share their snack,
It's a party on the branch, no lack!

A badger stirs, yawning wide,
And finds a feather, oh what a ride!
He slips and slides, oh what a mess,
But laughter lives in every guess.

The sun dips low, the colors dance,
As fireflies twinkle, giving a chance.
Join the crew, friendly and spry,
In our joyful nest, watch spirits fly.

As day turns night, and stars take flight,
Every creature shares delight.
With every smile, with every jest,
This is our home, we are truly blessed.

Mirthful Moments in the Trees

Squirrels wear hats made of leaves,
Chasing their shadows, oh how it deceives.
Chirps of the birds blend with giggles,
As branches dance like wiggly wiggles.

A raccoon tells jokes with a wink and a grin,
While the turtles just chuckle, they can't keep it in.
The owls hoot with laughter, their eyes open wide,
As the sun setting low brings the jokes to abide.

Celestial Chatter in the Boughs

Up in the branches, where secrets reside,
The chatter of critters makes worries subside.
A fox in a top hat performs for the crowd,
While worms in their bow ties cheer out loud.

The sunbeams are tickling, the breeze carries fun,
As laughter erupts from the paws and the bun.
Even the old trees join in on the skit,
Rustling their leaves, they contribute wit.

Up High With a Smile

Rabbits hop high, with a bounce and a twist,
Each leap sparkles bright, none dare to resist.
The chipmunks play tag as they scurry around,
While butterflies giggle without making a sound.

A party of squirrels holds a dance on the bough,
With acorns for drums, 'tis a wild, fun vow.
They spin and they twirl, with joy on display,
As laughter erupts, brightening the day.

Nature's Whimsical Whispers

In the canopy high, where the shadows frolic,
A woodpecker drums, his rhythm quite comical.
The ladybugs chuckle, their spots like confetti,
While frogs croak in chorus, their voices all ready.

The breeze tells a tale, of jokes on the wing,
As flowers eavesdrop and begin to sing.
With giggles and grins, nature too can play,
In this playful garden, joy leads the way.

Gales of Glee

In the branches, squirrels play,
Chasing shadows all the day,
With each leap, a giggle loud,
Making mischief, oh so proud.

Peeking down from leafy bows,
Raccoons dance, they steal the show,
Rolling acorns, tumbling free,
Laughter rides on every breeze.

A jay, with jokes so bright,
Cracks them under moonlight's light,
Every chuckle fills the air,
Joyful whispers everywhere.

In the glades, the stories weave,
Of the pranks that all believe,
Waves of glee among the trees,
Echoes carried by the breeze.

Harmony of the Hummingbirds

Tiny whirlwinds zip and zoom,
In their dance, there's joyful bloom,
With colors flashing everywhere,
Their laughter fills the summer air.

Fluttering near a blooming flower,
Sharing bright tales, hour by hour,
Darting quick, they slip and slide,
In a race, they won't collide.

Perched above, they pause to chat,
Wings a-dance, they laugh at that,
Each sweet nectar brings a cheer,
Chasing fun, they persevere.

Through the garden, giggles spread,
As little birds take flight instead,
In circles round, their joy ignites,
With melody that sparks delights.

Lively Legends in the Leaves

Whispers rustle in the green,
Tales of fun that can be seen,
What a giggle, what a cheer,
In every leaf, good vibes appear.

Woodpecker drumming on the bark,
Each tap a joke, a funny spark,
Swooping birds join in the fun,
Chasing beams of golden sun.

Caterpillars in a line,
Wiggle-wobble, oh so fine,
Cocooned dreams so bright and warm,
Soon they'll change, a new form born.

In the woods, where laughter flows,
Funny echoes sounds like prose,
With every rustle, a new tale,
In the leaves, the joys prevail.

The Jests of the Woodland Spirits

In the starlit glades, they tease,
Sprightly shadows, dancing with ease,
Whispers of fun in the night's embrace,
Each spirit enjoys the playful chase.

Mischief glimmers in their eyes,
With each trick, the laughter flies,
Soft giggles hidden in the dark,
Every rustle leaves a mark.

Chasing fireflies, they twirl and spin,
Crafting joy from deep within,
A riddle here, a jest over there,
Spreading laughter everywhere.

Through the trees, their laughter lingers,
Tickling leaves with playful fingers,
Mirthful moments, wild and free,
In the woods, they dance with glee.

Fluttering Fables in the Foliage

In the branches, stories sway,
As the breeze plays hide and seek.
A squirrel dons a cap of hay,
While a chipmunk dances, sleek.

A parrot jokes with a loud squawk,
Telling tales of silly fright.
Raccoons gather 'round to gawk,
At the antics of the night.

Leaves rustle with each giggle shared,
While the sun spills laughter bright.
Nature's stage, all unprepared,
Brings forth joy in pure delight.

So here beneath the verdant dome,
Where the wildest beings play,
Each fable weaves a tale of home,
Echoing the fun of the day.

Echoes of Merriment in the Meadow

In the meadow where daisies bloom,
Bumblebees buzz jokes with glee.
A frolicsome rabbit clears the room,
With a flip and a happy spree.

Grasshoppers leap with comic flair,
Hopping high in the warm sunlight.
They share a chuckle here and there,
As the butterflies take flight.

A mooing cow joins in the fun,
Tales of mischief in her voice.
Underneath the bright warm sun,
All unite to laugh and rejoice.

The laughter rings across the land,
Nature's giggles fill the air.
In this magical, funny strand,
Every creature joins the fair.

Raucous Revelries in the Treeline

High above in the swaying leaves,
Monkeys have thrown a grand parade.
Their costumes pop like autumn's eves,
As they dance in wild charade.

Owls sit wise in their cozy nook,
Laughing at the silliness below.
A silly dance for every look,
Crafted by the woodland show.

Frogs croak tunes on lily pads,
Serenading the jack-in-the-pulpit,
Amidst the giggles and happy fads,
Nature's beat makes spirits flit.

So join this raucous, leafy fest,
Where all of humor crowns the tree!
In wild revelry, we jest,
Each laugh spins joy, oh so free.

Squirrels' Serenade

Up in the branches, a soft serenade,
Squirrels chirp, making quite the sound.
They scurry about, no plans laid,
Chasing dreams on the ground they found.

With acorns tossed in playful jest,
They leap and twirl in the finest show.
Every jump is a cheerful quest,
Filling the glades where laughter flows.

A wise old owl shakes her head,
Chuckling at their endless spree.
"Keep it up, don't stop," she said,
"Life's too short for dull and dreary!"

As twilight woos the day away,
The forest hums a joyful tune.
In the trees where little creatures play,
Laughter dances beneath the moon.

The Sunlit Stage of Chirps

Tiny birds dance in the air,
With silly songs and a playful flair.
A squirrel flips with a twist and twirl,
While laughing leaves in the breeze unfurl.

A butterfly flutters, it giggles loud,
As ants march by, all perfectly proud.
The world is bright with this cheerful crew,
In the sunlit stage, we all enjoy the view.

Tales from the Leafy Theatre

In the leafy hall, a story unfolds,
Of a mischievous raccoon, so bold.
He stole some fruits, then ran in fright,
While the owls hooted with pure delight.

A rabbit slipped on the dewy grass,
With each little tumble, the giggles amass.
The trees hold secrets in their embrace,
Of laughter and joy in this charming place.

Giggling Under the Green

Under the branches, shadows flicker,
A frog makes jokes, and the tempo's quicker.
His croak is funny, a real delight,
As children laugh through the warm twilight.

A mouse tells tales of a close escape,
From the curious eyes of an unkind grape.
Giggles echo, they're hard to contain,
Under the green, joy's free from disdain.

Branches of Bliss

Swinging high, a squirrel's in glee,
Chasing shadows, so wild and free.
With each little leap, his antics shine,
In this paradise, everything's fine.

A chorus of critters, all join in song,
With whimsical tunes that just can't be wrong.
Branches of bliss cradle laughter's call,
In nature's embrace, joy is for all.

A Symphony of Swaying Green

In the branches, monkeys swing,
Chasing shadows that they bring.
With a laugh and playful shout,
They turn the calmness upside out.

Squirrels dance with acorn hats,
Juggling nuts like tiny brats.
Each leap brings a spark of joy,
Nature's own mischievous boy.

Birds chirp in a comical way,
Tickling leaves as they play.
A rhythm of nature's delight,
Echoes softly in the light.

Laughter rings through every tree,
Unveiling wonders wild and free.
In this green and vibrant scene,
Life's a merry, giggling routine.

Chronicles of the Whispering Woods

In the woods where whispers soar,
Stories dance on every floor.
A rabbit winks with gleeful pride,
As giggles echo, side by side.

Trees tell jokes, their branches sway,
Rooted laughter here to stay.
Silly shadows skip and prance,
Inviting all to join the dance.

Breezes carry secrets round,
Tickling leaves without a sound.
The mushrooms chuckle, soft and round,
While squirrels stash their jokes profound.

With every breeze, a tale unfolds,
Of playful spirits, brave and bold.
Laughter weaves through twinkling light,
In the woods, joy takes its flight.

Playful Spirits of the Forest

Dancing leaves in breezy cheer,
Tiny spirits gather near.
Chasing sunlight, whisking by,
With twinkling eyes that touch the sky.

The forest floor is their stage,
Behind each tree, a hiding page.
Echoes of laughter fill the air,
As they frolic without care.

A deer with a jaunty hat,
A clever fox, a playful cat.
In every nook, a jest is found,
As giggles spin and whirl around.

Their antics spark delight and glee,
Underneath the great green tree.
Here joy thrives and mischief reigns,
As the playful spirits entertain.

Moments of Merriment in the Mist

Morning mist wraps round the pines,
Hiding secrets, playfull signs.
The rabbits giggle, leap and hide,
As whispers dance from side to side.

A foggy prank, a sneaky breeze,
Rustles branches with such ease.
With every turn, surprises bloom,
Filling the air with joyful gloom.

A crow caws loud with playful glee,
Mocking shadows, wild and free.
While a turtle in slow motion,
Joins the laughter like a potion.

In this land of whimsy bright,
Where laughter twinkles in the light,
Moments wrap us in their bliss,
In the mist, it's joy we kiss.

Whispers of the Canopy

In the rustling leaves, a jest is born,
Squirrels giggle, their acorns are scorned.
A wise owl hoots with a wink and a grin,
Telling tales of chases he'd surely win.

The tall trees sway, the branches cheer,
As monkeys swing, their laughter's quite near.
A parrot squawks jokes, perched high in the shade,
While shadows dance lightly, a playful charade.

A breeze tickles feathers, a playful breeze,
Laughter floats by, carried with ease.
In every crack and creak, there's fun,
Moments of joy under the sun.

So gather your friends, enjoy the show,
Nature's own circus, where giggles flow.
With each whispered secret of fun from above,
The canopy grins, full of whimsy and love.

Chasing Sunbeams Among the Leaves

Golden rays peek through the emerald green,
Tiny tots chase light, a magical scene.
With giggles and shrieks, they dance around,
While shadows play tricks on the playful ground.

Fireflies twinkle like stars in the day,
While silly little critters come out to play.
Each twirl and leap, a contagious delight,
As laughter rings clear in the warm summer light.

A butterfly flutters, teasing a race,
While a turtle chuckles, slow in his pace.
The sun smiles down, casting warmth all around,
In a world woven with joy, merriment found.

So leap through the patches of dappled sun,
Join in the laughter; let's all have fun!
For in every glimmer, a story unfolds,
Of giggles and glee, and mischief retold.

The Giggle Grove

In the heart of the grove, where the giggles grow,
Tiny critters gather, putting on a show.
A hedgehog juggles with berries galore,
And the rabbits all chuckle, wanting more.

With a tap-dancing frog on a lily so bright,
Their laughter is magic, pure delight.
Giggling in chorus, they sing to the sky,
While the breeze carries whispers as it floats by.

A dance party starts with a bashful old hare,
Who twirls and then stumbles, causing great flair.
The trees join in, swaying to the tune,
As laughter erupts, cradled by the moon.

So come join the fun, in this whimsical land,
Where every leaf giggles, hand in hand.
In the grove where chuckles echo all day,
We'll celebrate joy, come laugh and play!

Secrets of the Swaying Boughs

High in the branches, secrets unfold,
Swaying like stories, both funny and bold.
A raccoon in costume, a cap and a tie,
Pretends it's a king, oh my, oh my!

The wind starts to whistle a silly tune,
As birds chirp choruses beneath the moon.
Swinging with glee on the rope of a vine,
A delightful parade of fun intertwines.

Nuts drop with a thud, creating quick laughs,
While the young chipmunks do their silly staff.
Under the arches of laughter, we trot,
Discovering giggles in each little spot.

So open your heart to nature's sly cheer,
With every small chuckle, let joy reappear.
For the boughs share their secrets, both quirky and bright,

Let's dance in the shadows, from morning to night!

Harmony of the High Hues

Up in the branches where squirrels play,
Chasing each other all through the day.
A parrot squawks jokes, oh what a sight,
While woodpeckers drum with all of their might.

A sloth hangs around, moves at a crawl,
While the raccoon belly flops, making a call.
The laughter rings out, a melodious cheer,
In this leafy haven, there's nothing to fear.

The breeze carries giggles from little bird beaks,
While the owl just rolls his eyes, playing the Greeks.
With every tickle of leaves in the air,
Life in the high hues is beyond compare.

So come join the romp, leave your worries behind,
Where nature's own laugh is the best you will find.
Every chirp and each rustle helps create a song,
In a world full of joy, where we all belong.

Lighthearted Legends of the Leafage

In a leafy theatre where shadows play,
A wise old turtle cracks jokes in his way.
The bumblebees buzz with a beat so sweet,
As butterflies dance on their little light feet.

A mischievous monkey steals all the snacks,
While a chipmunk jumps, causing laugh-tastic flacks.
Leaves whisper secrets of playful delight,
And the sun sets slowly, ending the flight.

The stories are tall, and the laughter is wide,
With friends in the trees all laughing with pride.
Beneath twisting branches, they gather and tell,
Of mischief and antics where everyone fell.

So gather your pals, lean back, take a peek,
To the lighthearted stories, the fun, and the cheek.
In a world made of giggles, all troubles just fade,
In the leafage's laughter, new memories are made.

The Froggy Figment's Frolic

In the pond's cool embrace, a froggy does leap,
With dreams of grand tales, he's jumping so deep.
His friends laugh aloud at his wild little spins,
Creating a splash, turning frowns into grins.

The dragonflies giggle and zoom all around,
While the fish in the water flip-up with a sound.
Each croak becomes part of a silly old tune,
Beneath the bright, whirling, and whimsical moon.

A turtle spins tales of the great and the grand,
While grasshoppers join in, a colorful band.
Every leap and each story fills the air with delight,
In the froggy's fair realm, everything feels right.

So hop into fun, don't miss out on the cheer,
With froggy figments, there's nothing to fear.
Let laughter ring out as they dance in a line,
To the rhythm of nature—what a joyful design!

Aerial Anecdotes

From the heights of the trees, watch the world below,
Where gathering creatures put on a show.
A squirrel in spandex, a sight quite absurd,
Telling tall tales that no one else heard.

The winds bring a chorus of giggles and glee,
As the owls in the night tell of funny old trees.
A dance breaks out under the silver-lit skies,
With shadows and laughter, the night never dies.

A friendly old crow shares a riddle or two,
While fireflies flicker, competing in hue.
Chirping with joy, the crickets conclude,
That tales of the night are best shared in a mood.

So fly with the whispers of friends in the air,
Join in the tales, let go of your care.
With smiling companions and stories so bright,
Aerial anecdotes will light up the night.

Delight in the Arboreal Tales

In branches high, where laughter grows,
The squirrels dance in funny clothes.
With acorns tossed, and giggles shared,
They swing and whirl, none seems impaired.

A wise old crow, with witty quips,
Tells jokes that make the tree bark chip.
While rabbits roll in grass below,
A parade of pals steals the show.

The branches sway with every joke,
As ants parade in hats bespoke.
A whisper rustles through the leaves,
The humor twists, and all believes.

In vibrant hues, the world's a stage,
With every bark, there's a laugh-age.
So join this fest where trees await,
In tales of joy, they celebrate.

The Frolicsome Nature's Nook

An owl in specs reads with flair,
As mice in tuxes promptly stare.
Their tiny giggles fill the air,
In nature's nook, they know no care.

Fluttering leaves play hide and seek,
With beetles dressed in costumes chic.
A rabbit juggles berries bright,
The laughter echoes, pure delight.

The breezes swirl with jokes enshrined,
A dance of whimsy, sweetly twined.
As chubby raccoons share the tales,
With playful spins and gleeful wails.

So come and join this wild ballet,
Where critters frolic, sing and play.
In every nook, joy finds a way,
The heart delights, come seize the day.

The Spirit of the Sylvan Smile

Beneath the boughs, the chitchat flows,
With little sprites in cheeky clothes.
The woodpecker drums a silly beat,
As giggles echo, oh so sweet.

Mischievous foxes scheme and plot,
A game of pranks, they give a shot.
While hedgehogs roll in fits of glee,
Their laughter spreads from tree to tree.

A raccoon jests, with playful flair,
Sells dreams of cookies in mid-air.
The fireflies twinkle, laughing bright,
As night unfolds with sheer delight.

In forests deep, the merriment swells,
A chorus of giggles, friendly yells.
So come and bask in this warm glow,
The spirit's laughter steals the show.

Revel in the Rustic Arboretum

Where branches twist in playful jest,
And woodland critters are the best.
The turtles race, though slow they seem,
While every leaf begins to beam.

A dancing bear, in floppy hat,
Tells stories that make all fall flat.
With every tale, a happy cheer,
The rustic charm draws us near.

As bees buzz by with puns so sweet,
The flowers bloom to the rhythm of feet.
The thrill of joy fills every space,
With nature's grin upon each face.

So come and join this merry crew,
With laughter ringing, spirits brew.
In woody realms, we find our place,
Where smiles abound, and hearts embrace.

The Glee within the Grain

In the trunks where squirrels dance,
They spin and twirl in happy prance.
With acorns as hats, they frolic about,
Creating giggles, a joyful shout.

Branches bend with their silly tricks,
A game of tag, they dive and flick.
The breeze carries their chuckles high,
While leaves rustle like laughter in the sky.

A woodpecker drums a lively beat,
As critters join with tiny feet.
A chorus of squeaks resounds in the air,
In the laughter-filled haven they share.

Amidst the bark and vibrant green,
A world of mirth unfolds unseen.
These merry moments, pure and bright,
In nature's embrace, a sheer delight.

Echoes of Enchantment in the Canopy

High above where the sunlight plays,
The whispers of joy fill the balmy days.
A parrot jests with a colorful flair,
While babbling brooks join the fun in the air.

Underneath the leaves, lighthearted banter,
A rabbit hops with a playful canter.
The shadows dance with twinkling eyes,
While butterflies flutter, giggling in disguise.

Between the branches, giggles collide,
As frogs croak jokes from the muddy slide.
Each chirp and trill a playful tune,
Under the watchful gaze of the moon.

With every rustle, a tale unfolds,
In the vibrant press where laughter beholds.
In this verdant realm where joy will abide,
Echoes ripple wide, a whimsical ride.

A Canvas of Cheer

Beneath a sky brushed with laughter's hue,
The paint-splattered trees break the morning dew.
Each branch is a brush dancing in glee,
Creating art where the happy hearts flee.

A jolly old raccoon in a bandit hat,
Steals moments of fun, and where's he at?
With echoes of joy swirling all around,
In this vibrant gallery, happiness found.

Sunbeams paint patterns on playful leaves,
Where mischief brews, and the fun never leaves.
The colors of chuckles waft through the air,
As nature's humor spreads everywhere.

In this lively orchard of smiles galore,
Every step brings laughter, a vibrant tour.
With hearts wide open, we dance through the cheer,
A canvas of joy that we hold so dear.

Swaying Smiles in the Sycamores

In the sycamores where laughter flows,
Giggling leaves dance in a playful prose.
Branches sway with a rhythmic tease,
While breezes tickle like cheerful bees.

The acorn brigade stirs up a prank,
With nutty jokes at their little bank.
A chipmunk grins, plotting his spree,
In a world where sunshine sets spirits free.

As shadows sway and sunlight beams,
The forest echoes with playful dreams.
Each rustle and chuckle, a sweet little song,
In this haven of joy where we all belong.

Beneath the branches, in nature's embrace,
Laughter, a treasure, we gleefully chase.
With each heartfelt giggle, our spirits ignite,
In the swaying trees where the world feels right.

Mirth Under the Moonlit Branches

In the branches where shadows dance,
Squirrels giggle, taking a chance.
Owls with spectacles laugh so bright,
Chasing fireflies through the night.

Raccoons in masks, oh what a sight,
Playing tag in lantern light.
Whispers of joy in every nook,
With a book of giggles, they all took.

A frog jokes low, a cricket sings,
Nature's laughter, oh how it rings!
Jumping jays crack silly quips,
As the moonlight on friendship drips.

Beneath the stars, their stories twine,
In the heart of the boughs, magic aligns.
When joy takes flight on gentle breeze,
Laughter echoes through the trees.

Whims of the Woodland

A chipmunk with a hat too grand,
Swaps wild jokes with a wise old band.
Frolicking laughter fills the air,
As each critter shares a tale rare.

The raccoon's prank with shiny things,
Sets off giggles and wild flings.
Even the pines sway with glee,
In the arms of playful jubilee.

Playful hedgehogs roll in mirth,
Chasing their shadows, giving birth.
To laughter round like falling leaves,
In every crack, the forest weaves.

A dance, a twirl, the fun won't end,
As woodland pals all come to blend.
In the heart of the joyful wood,
Happiness flows like a bubbling flood.

Cascading Chuckles

A babbling brook, a giggling glee,
Where splashes tell tales, wild and free.
Each ripple carries a story's scent,
Of chuckles shared and time well spent.

Bees buzzing low, they share a prank,
On unsuspecting leaves they clank.
With honey's sweet taste and a wink,
They dance by the waters, quick as ink.

Bouncing bunnies in a never-ending chase,
Hop over puddles, a lively race.
Every leap springs a joyful sound,
Echoing laughter, all around.

Mischief erupts as the sun sinks low,
Golden moments put on a show.
In the heart of nature's embrace,
Laughter ripples, a joyous trace.

The Grins of High-Dwelling Creatures

On branches high, where the sunlight gleams,
Monkeys swing, bursting at the seams.
With playful shouts and clever tricks,
Their laughter rolls like comic flicks.

A parrot squawks in vibrant hues,
Telling tales that tease and amuse.
The clouds above nod in delight,
To the echoes of joy taking flight.

Night owls perched on posts so clear,
Hold their breath, then burst with cheer.
With every whoop and every clap,
Their giggles form a cozy map.

As daylight wanes, the fun remains,
In every nook, where laughter reigns.
With every chortle from up on high,
The forest joins in, oh my, oh my!

The Dance of the Dappled Sunlight

Beneath the trees, shadows prance,
A squirrel tumbles, takes a chance.
A rustling leaf shouts, "Look at me!"
As laughter rings out, wild and free.

The daisies sway with giggling glee,
While buzzing bees play hide and seek.
A chubby owl with a puzzled frown,
Wonders why the world spins round.

Playful winds tease the fluffy clouds,
A chorus of cheers from merry crowds.
The sunlight winks, a jest to share,
Making shadows dance with flair.

In this realm where joy takes flight,
The critters revel, hearts so light.
Joking whispers weave through the air,
Nature's laughter everywhere.

Jests in the Forest Canopy

Underneath the leafy cover,
A raccoon slips, it starts to hover.
A monkey swings, a playful show,
"Catch me if you can!" he will crow.

The crickets chirp a cheeky tune,
As butterflies dance, a bright festoon.
A fox attempts to leap and land,
But grows dizzy, stumbles, and stands.

Giggles echo through the trees,
As chipmunks tell their funny keys.
Each branch a stage, the woodland crew,
Performs their antics, never through.

A playful breeze whispers, "Ha!"
While squirrels plot their nutty plot.
In this place where laughs collide,
Nature's humor cannot hide.

Tales from the Elevated Branches

On high above, the stories weave,
Where giggling birds never leave.
A parrot cracks a silly jest,
While owls in robes look quite impressed.

With plenty of snickers from the throng,
A woodpecker drums a quirky song.
A timid lizard, bold with flair,
Gestures grand, performs with care.

The skies burst forth with comic charms,
As honeybees buzz with open arms.
Each creature dupes, each creature pranks,
In this realm where laughter ranks.

From branches high to ground below,
The echoes of humor steal the show.
In every nook, a chuckle lives,
Where nature's tales, pure joy gives.

Frolics Under the Sky

Under the blue, the games begin,
A playful breeze invites a spin.
Rabbits hop in a merry chase,
While all around, the sun leaves trace.

Crickets leap on leafy plates,
As laughter rolls like bouncing mates.
With every twist and every turn,
The forest glows, the colors burn.

A bear who thinks he's quite the star,
Attempts to dance; he isn't far.
A tumble here, a roll or two,
While squirrels cheer, "You did great too!"

In wild delight, the creatures play,
Creating joy both night and day.
From gentle whispers under trees,
Our hearts are lifted, aiming to please.

Joyful Jives of the Woodland Critters

Squirrels dance with acorn hats,
They spin and twirl on twiggy mats.
Bunnies hop with silly grace,
Chasing tails in a wild race.

Chirpy birds sing tunes so sweet,
With wobbly steps, they tap their feet.
A hedgehog rolls and starts to giggle,
While frogs jump high and give a wiggle.

The fox joins in with a merry cheer,
Wagging its tail, spreading good cheer.
Raccoons juggle shiny stones,
With joyful jests, they toss and moan.

In the shadows, the weasel pranks,
As laughter echoes, the forest thanks.
Caught in a whirlwind of playful blight,
The woodland critters dance through the night.

The Spectacle of Sundrenched Laughter

Sunbeams stream through leafy crowns,
As giggles rise without any frowns.
A playful breeze pulls at their tails,
While raccoons spin in colorful trails.

Down by the brook, the frogs convene,
With splashes and croaks, they're quite the scene.
They leap and dive with goofy flair,
Sending ripples through warm summer air.

The butterflies flutter with dazzling grace,
Each twist and turn a curious race.
Chipmunks squeak, their cheeks piled high,
With treasures stashed, oh me, oh my!

Mischievous ants march in a line,
Playing tag on a sun-drenched vine.
The laughter rings, a joyous sound,
As woodland friends play all around.

Whispers Among the Leaves

Whispers tickle through the green,
As critters frolic, oh what a scene!
A joyful breeze carries their plays,
Filling the air with laughter's rays.

Little mice in a playful chase,
Scurry about, no time to waste.
With tiny giggles and squeaky glee,
They sneak past the maple with utmost glee.

Chirping wings in a feathery rush,
As partridges dance with a joyous hush.
A deer prances with a playful grin,
As the laughter spins, it twirls right in.

Amidst the trees where shadows dwell,
Silly tales are woven well.
In every rustle and every breeze,
Laughter blooms among the leaves.

Giggles in the Canopy

Up in the branches, the joys reside,
Where monkeys swing and laughter won't hide.
With cheeky smiles, they leap and play,
In a jolly game throughout the day.

The parrots squawk with a colorful shout,
As they steal grapes, there's giggles about.
A squirrel slips, then starts to roll,
In a fit of giggles, the whole troop's goal.

Bouncing berries, oh what a sight,
As critters scurry with sheer delight.
With each clumsy tumble, a chuckle breaks,
In this canopy of joy, laughter awakes.

As shadows dance in the fading light,
The cozy chatter rings through the night.
In the canopy high, the fun won't cease,
Under the stars, they find their peace.

Riddles in the Boughs

A squirrel asked a wise old crow,
"Why do the leaves dance to and fro?"
The crow just cawed, with a wink so sly,
"Because they're laughing as the breezes fly!"

A chipmunk chuckled, his cheeks so round,
"The acorns roll when I'm not around!"
A giggle echoed through the trees,
"Catch me if you can!" said the playful breeze.

A fox joined in, with a grin so wide,
"Why do trees wear bark like a hide?"
The answer danced, buzzing like a bee,
"Because they've got secrets that are wild and free!"

The laughter rose, a sweet serenade,
The forest glowed, in sunshine it played.
With riddles afloat, and mischief in the air,
Nature's funny whispers were everywhere!

Frolicsome Friends of the Forest

In the heart of the woods, where giggles ignite,
A rabbit jumps high, oh what a sight!
He tickles a fox, who rolls on the ground,
With every hop and skip, joy abounds.

A hedgehog spun tales, his quills in a twist,
"Did you hear the one about the fish who wished?"
The friends gathered 'round, laughter to share,
As leaves rustled softly, like giggles in air.

An owl hooted loudly, so wise and so bright,
"What's a tree's favorite game at night?"
They pondered and pondered, then shrieked with glee,
"Hide and seek with the stars, oh can't you see?"

With laughter like music, the forest would sing,
A gathering of friends, in a whimsical ring.
Frolicsome spirit, in every heart's glow,
These playful companions, forever will flow!

Jollification Overhead

Above the meadow, where the birds play,
Chirping a tune that lifts the gray.
A little bluebird slipped on a vine,
His flapping and flailing, oh how divine!

The butterflies giggled, a beautiful sight,
"Oh dear feathered friend, hold on tight!"
They fluttered around in a whimsical flight,
Encouraging laughter to take its height.

A mischievous breeze came dancing by,
Tickling the feathers of birds in the sky.
With every swoop, the giggles grew loud,
In this jollification, a jubilant crowd!

As sunbeams shimmered through branches so green,
They spread joyful warmth, as laughter was seen.
High over the ground, where fun takes its stand,
Jollity sparkles just like grains of sand.

Songs of Serenity and Smile

In the hush of the woods, where shadows play,
The breezes sang softly at the end of day.
A calm little brook, so clear and so bright,
Whispered of magic in the fading light.

Beneath the tall trees, a chorus began,
Of crickets and frogs, a whimsical plan.
With each little croak, laughter would swell,
In nature's own symphony, all was well.

A playful raccoon with a grin so wide,
Juggled some berries with a glint in his eye.
"Catch me if you can, or try if you dare!"
The forest erupted in giggles of air.

As twilight descended, the stars took their place,
The moon shared her light, a gentle embrace.
In songs of serenity, where smiles unite,
Nature's own laughter spread warmth through the night.

Songs of Serenity and Smile

In the hush of the woods, where shadows play,
The breezes sang softly at the end of day.
A calm little brook, so clear and so bright,
Whispered of magic in the fading light.

Beneath the tall trees, a chorus began,
Of crickets and frogs, a whimsical plan.
With each little croak, laughter would swell,
In nature's own symphony, all was well.

A playful raccoon with a grin so wide,
Juggled some berries with a glint in his eye.
"Catch me if you can, or try if you dare!"
The forest erupted in giggles of air.

As twilight descended, the stars took their place,
The moon shared her light, a gentle embrace.
In songs of serenity, where smiles unite,
Nature's own laughter spread warmth through the night.

Bark and Banter

In the shade where shadows play,
Trees share secrets, come what may.
Leaves rustle with a giggling sound,
Nature's jokes in circles found.

A squirrel with a nut so round,
Dances fast, leaps off the ground.
The branches shake, a playful cheer,
Echoes laughter, drawing near.

A woodpecker taps an amusing beat,
While ants march in a funny fleet.
Life above brings joys galore,
Each bark opened, reveals more.

In the rustle, in the croak,
Every creature knows a joke.
Under the boughs, they all relate,
In this grove, they celebrate.

Chasing Sunbeams in the Breezes

Sunbeams bouncing, oh so bright,
Chasing shadows, pure delight.
Blades of grass like tickles rise,
Breezes whisper, tickle, and surprise.

The flowers giggle with each sway,
While butterflies join in the play.
A little rabbit hops with glee,
Trying to catch the light, you see!

Wobbly bees buzz and dance,
Joining in the sunny prance.
Through the field, the laughter flows,
In the warmth, joy only grows.

Every creature finds their fun,
Underneath the smiling sun.
With the breeze, their spirits soar,
Chasing sunlight evermore.

The Mischief of Squirrels

Squirrels dart from tree to tree,
With wiggly tails so wild and free.
Sneaking snacks with a cheeky grin,
In the park, let the mischief begin!

Chasing each other round the trunk,
Over roots, they leap and punk.
With acorns held in tiny paws,
They giggle, never stopping for a pause.

One steals a hat, the other twirls,
Around the branches, they give a whirl.
Jumping high, they tease and play,
Making even the grumpiest sway.

From high above, they watch the ground,
Belly laughs in knots abound.
With every leap, they make a scene,
The tree's their stage, their world, their dream.

Laughter Echoes in the Woods

In the heart of woods so deep,
Laughter dances, never sleeps.
A chorus of giggles fills the air,
Every creature joins the flair.

The owl hoots a wise old joke,
While frogs croak laughter like a cloak.
The rustling leaves join in the fun,
As sunlight glimmers, one by one.

A jumpy fawn trips on a root,
Spinning round in a playful suit.
The chipmunks snicker at the show,
Playing pranks, their favorite flow.

With every rustle, squeak, and cheer,
Echoes ring, they bring good cheer.
In the woods, where joy takes flight,
Laughter dances, pure delight.

Playful Poetry of the Wild

In the green, a squirrel leaps,
Wearing acorn hats, it peeps.
A rabbit giggles, hops in line,
While frogs play songs and drink some wine.

A parrot squawks a funny tune,
Dancing to the light of the moon.
The raccoons join, a band so grand,
With maracas made of soft, warm sand.

The bushes rustle, a fox rolls by,
Chasing butterflies that flutter high.
The bees buzz jokes, they all agree,
Today's no day for misery!

Leaves laugh softly, sharing their cheer,
As the sun shines bright, bringing all near.
With each giggle, life feels so right,
In this wild place of pure delight.

Rhapsody of Rustling Leaves

Underneath the leafy dome,
A chipmunk makes his furry home.
He tells tall tales of nuts so big,
While caterpillars dance a jig.

The sun tickles the grass below,
As snails slide by, moving slow.
A twirling leaf, it takes a chance,
Inviting all to join the dance.

The wise old owl begins to laugh,
At squirrels arguing – 'I saw it last!'
With a wink, he shares his sight,
Of all the antics through the night.

In a bush, a fox lays low,
Watching as the giggles flow.
With a flick, he joins the spree,
And laughter fills the wood with glee.

Stories of the Whispering Woods

In the heart where shadows play,
A bunny tells a joke each day.
The trees whisper secrets, oh so sly,
As fireflies wink and flutter by.

A crow sings melodies, quite absurd,
With punchlines that are rarely heard.
The little ants march in a line,
With hats of leaves, they look so fine!

A hedgehog rolls in playful spins,
While crickets chirp and join the wins.
The lizard laughs, his tail held high,
"What's a tree's favorite drink? Root beer!" he cries.

As sunbeams tickle the mossy floor,
Each laugh bounces, asking for more.
In nature's realm, the joy abounds,
As friendship echoes, laughter sounds.

Joyful Skits in the Arbor

In the nook where the branches bend,
A cast of critters, all good friends.
The playful bear rehearses a show,
While butterflies flutter to and fro.

A raccoon dons a silly wig,
Pretending to dance, oh so big!
The hedgehog joins with funny moves,
In the spotlight, the laughter grooves.

The parrot tells quirky tales so bright,
As the sun settles down, painting the night.
With acorn cups and berry pies,
The woodland cheers, oh how they rise!

The final bow, they share a grin,
With echoes of joy, they soak it in.
In the arbor, where fun runs free,
Each heart sings in harmony.

Silliness Among the Foliage

In the branches, giggles soar,
Squirrels dance, then drop and roar.
Leaves chuckle, rustling in the breeze,
As playful winds tease with ease.

Birds wear hats, they flap and spin,
One fell down with a silly grin.
Raccoons hide, peeking just a bit,
While butterflies flicker, doing a split.

Laughter echoes through the trees,
Bouncing high, like honey bees.
Each branch holds a secret joke,
As wise old owls secretly poke.

When night falls, stars join the fun,
Winking down, the laughter's begun.
Naughtiness drapes like a blanket wide,
In the woods, where giggles abide.

Secrets of the Skyward Friends

Chirps and chortles fill the air,
Clouds giggle, light as a feather.
A raccoon's mask, so sly with flair,
In shadows, they hold laughter together.

The wise old owl, with a wink,
Shares tales of a sneezy pink flamingo.
While starlings dip and dive in sync,
Chasing each other with zesty bingo.

The breezy gossip of playful winds,
Twists and dances, no pair is shy.
With every flip, a tale begins,
Of silly pranks beneath the sky.

Hopping from branch to branch with cheer,
Friends laugh at the quirks they see.
In the skyward kingdom, joy is near,
As secrets unfold, wild and free.

The Glee of the Nesting Birds

In cozy nests, they chirp and play,
With worms as treats, in disarray.
Feathery hats and bright, bold beaks,
They swap funny stories, giggling peaks.

A little one trips on a twig,
And lands right in a puddle, big!
All their friends burst into song,
As splashes and laughter last so long.

With flapping wings, they twirl and glide,
Like silly dancers, they take pride.
Each tock and each tick of the day,
Brings cheerful moments, come what may.

As dusk falls down, they share a dream,
Of mischief and games, their laughter's theme.
Nesting birds, with hearts so light,
Sing their silliness into the night.

Frolics in the Upper Realm

High above, where the tall trees sway,
Mischief reigns both night and day.
Chipmunks dart, a fuzzy brigade,
Turning acorns into a charade.

A chipmunk shows off a new dance,
With a twist and a silly prance.
The wind joins in with a gentle tease,
Tickling feathers, putting minds at ease.

Giggling leaves flaunt their green attire,
As butterflies flirt, lifting higher.
In this realm, laughter's the game,
And every critter knows their name.

When the sun dips low and the moon awakes,
Echoes of joy the night gently takes.
From branches above, the chorus resounds,
In the upper realm, joy astounds!

The Merriment of Mossy Friends

In the shade where the mossies play,
Squirrels dance in a silly display.
They chase their tails, a comical sight,
Chirping jokes until the night.

Beneath the pines, a gnome does cheer,
Telling tales from yesteryear.
With each punchline, the mushrooms snicker,
While fireflies flicker, getting quicker.

A rabbit rolls with laughter loud,
Joining in with a giggling crowd.
Frogs hop along, in a merry groove,
As every one finds their silly move.

The sky shakes with joyful noise,
While crafty raccoons play with toys.
Under the branches, they feel so spry,
In a circle of fun, oh my, oh my!

Laughing Leaves in a Breeze

Rustling leaves with a cheeky grin,
Whispering secrets of where they've been.
Breezes chuckle, tickling the air,
Spreading giggles everywhere.

The owls wink from their cozy perch,
While playful winds take the leafy search.
They spin and twirl, in a whirl of cheer,
Giggling softly for all to hear.

A cheeky squirrel wears acorn hats,
While dancing with friends—the clever rats.
They gather 'round for a riddle fest,
As laughter blooms from every nest.

The sun beams down, a bright spotlight,
On antics played with pure delight.
And as they prance in joyful tease,
Nature smiles at this funny breeze.

Folklore from the Green Expanse

In the heart of a forest, tales unfold,
Of daring deeds and mischief bold.
A songbird sings of a rogue, quite sly,
Who made the bees drop honey from the sky.

A turtle tells of a race so grand,
With a hare who thought he'd rule the land.
But hiccuping laughter, like a snort,
Made the crowd chuckle at his retort.

The elder oak shares secrets deep,
With stories that make the critters weep.
As wise old tales curl around like vines,
Creating smiles in all designs.

The buzz of laughter fills the air,
In this land of fun, so rare.
Every creature joins the jest,
In this green expanse, they're truly blessed.

Whistle of the Winds and Wonders

The winds whistle tunes of glee,
As they rustle through each lofty tree.
Not a creature quiet on this day,
For giggles soar and frolic, at play.

The fox prances, a dance so fine,
While crickets chirp in perfect line.
Each note a chuckle from grassy mound,
As laughter echoes all around.

The owl hoots a riddle from night,
While everyone gathers, eager for a bite.
With branches shaking and leaves alight,
The whispers of joy brim with delight.

As dusk arrives and stars peek through,
The woodland doors feel bright and new.
With a final laugh and a playful spin,
They bid goodnight, until fun begins!

The Humor of the Twilight Woods

In the woods at dusk's embrace,
A squirrel danced with funny grace.
He tripped on roots and made a face,
  Then giggled softly, in his place.

A wise old owl, with glasses bright,
  Joked about the lost daylight.
His feathery friends were such a sight,
  Swaying to the moon's first light.

The fox tried to sing a tune,
But sounded more like a swooning baboon.
Laughter echoed through the gloom,
  As shadows danced like a cartoon.

In every nook, a joke was spun,
The trees all leaned in, having fun.
With every laugh, the night begun,
  Twilight woods, a merry run.

Echoing Joys from Above

Up in the branches, a parrot yells,
"Got jokes to share, come hear my tales!"
With every squawk, the laughter swells,
As monkeys swing, shaking their shells.

A toucan painted bright with cheer,
Told funny stories loud and clear.
His silly beak brought lots of beer,
To all the birds who gathered near.

The breeze carried giggles far and wide,
As playful spirits danced with pride.
The patchwork leaves, they swayed and tried,
To catch the joy the skies had bide.

Each note of mirth, a sweet refrain,
From feathered friends and their crazy games.
A sky of joy, laughter untamed,
In echoing joy, they felt the same.

The Leafy Laughter Lounge

Under the leaves, a gathering spot,
Where every creature shared a lot.
The laughter spilled, a bubbling pot,
In the leafy lounge, they all forgot.

A rabbit juggled acorns with flair,
While hedgehogs rolled, without a care.
A playful raccoon made quite the snare,
With nods and winks, oh what a pair!

They passed around gossip, oh so thick,
With every tale, just one more trick.
The laughter burst, a joyous click,
As in their laughter, time would tick.

No worries there, just joyous sounds,
In the leafy lounge, friendship abounds.
With every laugh, the joy compounds,
In their little corner of leafy grounds.

Spirited Chirps in the Canopy

High in the trees where laughter teems,
A band of birds shared silly beams.
With chirps and tweets, filled with dreams,
They spun their tales like flowing streams.

A finch wore a hat that was way too big,
And danced around, doing a jig.
While sparrows hopped with quite the fig,
As laughter soared, just like a twig.

In the canopy, the sounds would ring,
As every creature joined to sing.
Their happy notes felt just like spring,
In spirited chirps, joy would cling.

The sun sneaked in, a golden ray,
As giggles chased the clouds away.
In cheerful chirps, they'd laugh and play,
In the vibrant world of the leafy ballet.

www.ingramcontent.com/pod-product-compliance
Lightning Source LLC
Chambersburg PA
CBHW071853160426
43209CB00003B/535